The Amazing Mr. Big

Kelly Fitzgerald Fowler

Illustrated by Bethany Smith

The Amazing Mr. Big

Published by Three Bird Press

Copyright 2015 Kelly Fitzgerald Fowler

Cover and interior illustrations by Bethany Smith

Copyright 2015

ALL RIGHTS RESERVED

No part of this publication may be reproduced, stored in a retrieval system or transmitted, in any form or by any means-electronic, mechanical, photocopying, recording or otherwise-without prior written permission. For permission requests write to the publisher, addressed "Attention Permission Coordinator," at the address below:

For information:

Three Bird Press

1121 Park West Blvd.

Suite B #125

Mt. Pleasant, SC 29466

Amazing Mr. Big: Kelly Fitzgerald Fowler.—1st ed.

ISBN-13 9780692457276

ISBN-10 0692457275

www.kellyfitzgeraldfowler.com

To the next generation:
Starting with
Abraham Wyatt Mitchell
and my future grandchildren.
Jesus and Gigi love you!

It really doesn't matter, as they disobeyed Mr. Big.

Genesis 2:17

He told them they could have the best and brightest fruit.

Genesis 2:16

The sickness we call sin was born from a disobeyed command.

Genesis 3:11

Until one day The Babe was born who carried peace within.

Isaiah 9:6

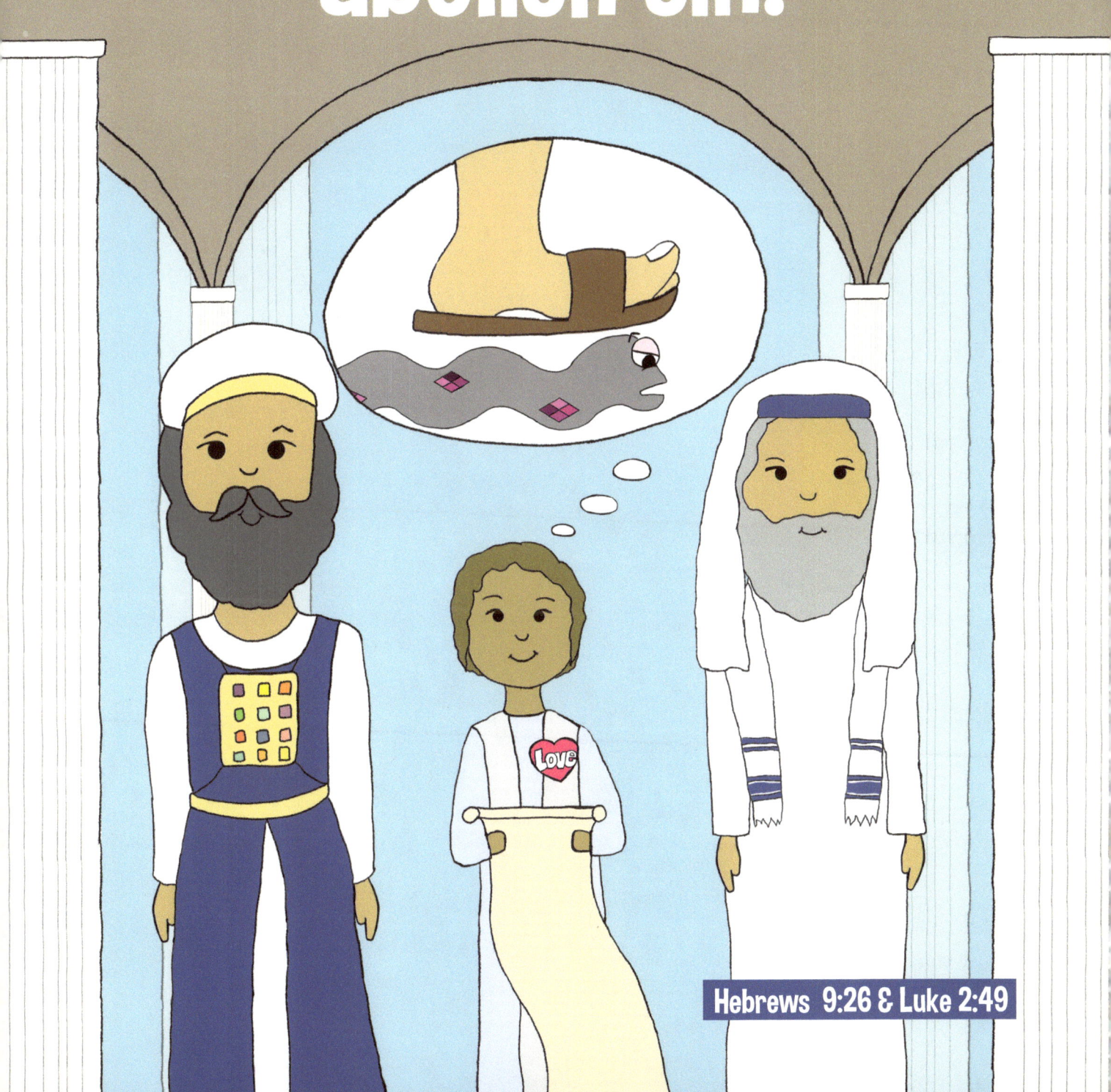

Mr. Big showed up and did not flinch as He knew that He had sent,

Isaiah 53 & Psalm 22

The Amazing Mr. Big

It could have been an apple; It may have been a fig.
It really doesn't matter, as they disobeyed Mr. Big.

He told them they could have the best and brightest fruit.
Politely, He was clear, but for her it did not suit.

She longed for the forbidden fruit. It was a dirty trick.
The reptile suggested it, and then it made her sick.

The sickness we call sin was born from a disobeyed command.
Not just her, the serpent thought, he also tricked the man.

Then they lived with sickness while waiting for relief.
The fruit that she had longed for had only brought them grief.

Until one day The Babe was born who carried peace within.
He grew and knew the secret was He would abolish sin.

The Babe, now a man, ready to pay and get the power back.
The serpent did not have a clue; he was about to get the sack.

Mr. Big showed up and did not flinch as He knew that He had sent,
His Son to die upon a cross so we could then repent.

The Son rose from the grave to everyone's surprise.
He conquered sin, and you can too instead of your demise.

So now you're free, to walk with God, The Amazing Mr. Big.
It really did not matter if it was an apple or a fig.